GARDEN WALKS

NEAR

BATH

Tim Mowl lectures on Architectural History and the English Landscape Garden in the department of History of Art at Bristol University. He is the author of several architectural studies, including a controversial life of John Wood the Elder of Bath and an indictment of post-war planning in the same city, *The Sack of Bath – And After*. His biographies of the Georgian aesthete-gardeners, Horace Walpole and William Beckford, were published in 1996 and 1998 respectively. *Country Walks Around Bath* has been in print since 1986, and there is a companion volume centred on Bristol. He is currently writing a social and cultural history of the gardeners and theorists who shaped the English landscape from 1630 to 1820.

Cover Illustration: The Pergola at Hestercombe

Why a GARDENER is the most extraordinary Man in the World.

Because no man has more business upon EARTH, and he always chuses good GROUNDS for what he does, he commands his THYME, he his master of the MINT, and fingers PENNY-ROYAL, he raises CELERY every year, and it is a bad year indeed, that does not bring him in a PLUMB, he meets with more BOUGHS than a Minister of state, he makes more BEDS than the French King & has in them more PAINTED LADIES, he makes RAKING his business more than his diversion, as many other gentlemen do; but makes it an advantage to his health and Fortune, which few others do, his Wife has enough of LADS LOVE & HEARTS EASE and never wishes for WEEDS. Distempers fatal to others never hurt him, he walks the better for the GRAVEL, and thrives most in a CONSUMPTION, his greatest pride, & the Worlds greatest envy, is, that he can have YEW when he pleases. An ADAMITE.

Tim Mowl's
GARDEN WALKS
NEAR
BATH

with illustrations by Janet Margrie

Millstream Books

for Gillian and Paul Sladen
Garden Enthusiasts

First published in 1999 by
Millstream Books, 18 The Tyning, Bath BA2 6AL

Set in Times New Roman and printed in Great Britain by
The Matthews Wright Press, Chard, Somerset

© text Tim Mowl 1999
© illustrations Janet Margrie 1999

ISBN 0948975547

Contents

Note that all opening times and entrance fees given in the text are those applying to 1999 and are, of course, liable to change.

Introduction

Not many books can be a sheer pleasure to write as this has been. Our angle of the South-West along the Severn and the Avon is quite unfairly well endowed with gardens. It may sound like boasting, but if you want to turn yourself into a reasonably well-informed garden historian then simply work your way, enjoyably but thoughtfully, through my ten gardens and I promise you will end up an expert arguing finer points with the best of them.

If it can be contrived, try to take the gardens chronologically to get the sequence of one fashion fading and another taking its place. Hardly any of the great formal seventeenth-century layouts have survived, but we have a perfect survivor at Westbury-on-Severn. Start there and move on to the informal Arcadian gardens at Prior Park and Stourhead. After Stourhead it would be impossible to improve on the eclectic style, but Painswick does delightfully miniaturise it and gets called 'Rococo' for no very good reasons. Blaise Castle grounds record the swing away from Classicism towards the painterly qualities of the Gothick Picturesque. Then, anyone with a feeling for the pre-Raphaelites will relish Stancombe with its rare, hidden garden and a pool from which you expect to see water nymphs reaching out their pale arms to pull Hylas in with them. I refer to that much reproduced painting by Waterhouse.

Iford Manor is the Edwardian garden in a more scholarly mood, something of an architectural museum with attendant plants. Edwin Lutyens and Gertrude Jekyll get the balance right again in favour of the flowers and the trees at Hestercombe, which pursues the theme of a rock garden to the sublime in its water rills. Great Chalfield was an interesting point of early twentieth-century indecision, then comes the Prince Charles-kitchen garden moderno at Barnsley House and we are back on our own home ground.

It was great going around some of these with my father, as he has that quality of open enthusiasm that a party of Americans will always show in a garden, but which groups of English visitors only rarely express. We are a reserved nation, but no one has told my father this, and I had to restrain him from stomping into Rosemary Verey's potager at Barnsley to pull the weeds out and from sampling apples on half the loaded espaliers at Westbury. Gardens affect people in a completely different way to houses. He would never try to dust Blenheim Palace or nick paintings from Wilton.

All four seasons work well with any of these ten, but do try for some sunshine as well as showers when you make a visit. Then with luck the entire pattern of our peculiar island aesthetics will unroll around you and you will end in a state of blissfully informed patriotism. So many people have tried so hard in the past to make places that enrich us. What will we have to offer apart from 'potagers' and gardens of remembrance?

My thanks go out to all those private owners, charitable trusts and civic custodians of gardens who have made such a book possible by their constant care and stewardship of this most fragile and fugitive of art forms. To my joint dedicatees I owe a debt of gratitude for their refined hospitality at Cambridge Place and their continuing encouragement of my literary ventures. Janet Margrie has produced a series of beautiful and evocative line drawings for the book which bring flooding back so many memories of the walks. Finally I should like to thank my father, my wife, my son and Brian Earnshaw for their walking company and my publisher, Tim Graham, for his enthusiasm for the subject and his professionalism in producing this book.

Tim Mowl, Bristol, Spring 1999

An Autumn Apple Garden
Strictly Regimented

Westbury Court Garden, Gloucestershire

Theme: A Dutch-inspired water garden of 1705 drawn by Jan Kip in 1712 and still at Westbury-on-Severn in a strange forgotten countryside of tidal excitements.

Directions: The journey there is, if you take the right road, as rewarding as the garden itself. Where, in overcrowded Britain, do forested hills roll down in dramatic valleys to a sea coast of shining sands, smuggler's creeks, abandoned ferry houses and lost hamlets untouched by the twentieth century? The answer is, not in Scotland or Wales, but in that north, Forest of Dean shore of the Severn estuary between Chepstow and Westbury. Neither the tourists nor the commuters have noticed one of England's most picturesque and atmospheric landscapes. True, those shining sands, which look golden in sunlight, are pure mud and dangerous to walk on, but that mud, with a little help from atomic power stations across the river, has kept this Severn shore real and unspoilt, no caravan parks and, except when the Severn bore roars up the narrowing channel, no surfers.

Pick a clear sunny day for wide views over glittering waters and you will be surprised and delighted by an unexpected riverine England. When you are on the M4 avoid the new French-built bridge over the river. Follow the signs for Chepstow (M48) and cross by the old (1966) suspension bridge with much better views. Turn off at Junction 22 for Chepstow, bypass the town dramatically and make for the A48 and Lydney. From then on it is scenic all the way, forest to the left, estuary to the right. Blakeney is finely sited but Newnham, half town, half village, is my favourite stop for coffee and antiques. Westbury Garden is at the far end of Westbury village. Turn right past the old people's home and park by the Tall Pavilion, where you will find the ticket kiosk.

On your way back, take your time; explore the peninsulas between road and river. They are clustered with high-sided, steep-roofed farm houses and cottages. Rodley and Awre are especially rich. Try for Gatcombe down lanes south-east of Blakeney.

Opening Times and Entrance Fees: The garden is open daily, except Monday and Tuesdays, from 27 March to 31 October, 11am-6pm. It is open on Bank Holiday Mondays but closed on Good Friday; £2.70 for adults, £1.35 for children. In the autumn the ticket kiosk may be unmanned, but there is an honesty box in the summerhouse wall. If you bring a packed lunch there is a discreet picnic area over the bridge on the far side of the stream, though I am sure that the original creators of the garden would have eaten in style on something like that handsome garden seat at the head of the canal. This is a memorial to Hugo Colchester-Wemyss (pronounced 'weems') 'the last of his family at Westbury Court'.

Things to look out for:
1   Mistletoe not far off ground level
2   A pear from the sixteenth century
3   Sash windows you would have problems raising
4   An entirely alien approach to gardening
5   Hedges of Lad's Love
6   One tree still flourishing which Kip refused to draw

Garden Tour:
    Play this garden the way its creators, Maynard Colchester I and his nephew, Maynard Colchester II, intended. Climb the steps of the Tall Pavilion, built in 1702-3 to a 'paterne' by a 'Mr Pyke', and there through the long windows you can see everything. This is not a garden for secrets; formal gardens of the late seventeenth century did not set out to imitate Nature but to discipline it. Everything is geometrical and laid out to be enjoyed at a glance. The long, 450 foot, 1696 canal immediately below you was the first Maynard Colchester's contribution; the other, T-shaped to the right, was his nephew's addition of around 1715. After that Westbury garden stood still, unchanged while almost every other

formal garden of this Dutch canal type in Britain was lost. The National Trust has hung a copy of Jan Kip's view of Westbury up on the wall; when you have absorbed that, you are ready for the garden's more subtle pleasures, so downstairs and out to the right.

There is no danger of getting lost in geometrical Westbury. From now on those two Colchesters will be controlling you from 300 years back. The old gentleman was a keen Christian: 'strictly pious himself & zealous to promote true Piety in others within his power', so his monument in the church says. His Amsterdam-born neighbour, Catherine Boevey of Flaxley Abbey, was another zealous Christian; the inspiration for these rigid yew hedges and straight canals probably came from her. With the sea to fight against and land to drain the Dutch could never afford our relaxed attitude to a kindly countryside. Originally that trim green lawn with the box spires between the two canals was a vegetable garden, all leeks and potatoes and cabbages, but that would hardly be National Trust, would it? Don't miss on your right a marvellous pollarded holm oak, four hundred years old. Kip missed it out of his view because it spoilt the symmetry.

As you turn left, back towards the road, you might want to inspect the Quincunx of small trees and clipped evergreens with its Dutch as opposed to French Parterre. The Colchesters' Tudor house stood where that gently naff old people's home has been built and the parterre which was laid out next to the house on the Kip has been copied here. Far more interesting is the walled garden ahead of you. I have enjoyed Westbury in Spring, Summer and Autumn, and it is the National Trust's replanting of the beds with the flowers and fruit trees listed in the Colchester accounts which makes the garden into a living lecture in 1707 scents, sights and flavours. Everything is carefully labelled and in October, my favourite visiting time, not only are the cyclamen all out, but windfall apples and pears strew the ground. Who cares about a few insect holes if you can nibble those tough sixteenth, seventeenth and eighteenth-century skins, so unlike the gaudy fruit in our supermarkets, and actually experience what the taste buds of William and Mary's reign savoured and valued? That, to me, really is the nearest to time travel we can ever hope to reach.

The walled garden, small as it is, takes time to explore. In Spring it has Queen Anne's Double Daffodil, weird auriculas and Persian Fritillaries; in Summer a shapeless yellow rose called Céline Forestier Noisette has the most authentic 'Jane Austen' perfume I have ever smelt. Whenever I come away from Westbury my fingers reek with a *pot-pourri* of all the leaves I have handled. Rue always lasts the longest. That gazebo with the fluted Corinthian pilasters is one of the Colchester nephew's additions. Unfortunately it is kept locked so you cannot enjoy the spectacle of passing traffic as the second Maynard Colchester would have done. Tastes change and the television has made gazebos superfluous.

Cross along the short side of the garden's rectangle. Neptune in the canal is supposed to have been found in the Severn mud after a wreck. An earlier statue of a little boy that sprayed water from a hand has been lost. The urns at the first *clairvoyée* are Colchester II, the pineapples at the second *clairvoyée* are Colchester I. It is at this point in the garden that you are most conscious of Westbury's bad luck with houses. If only there was a handsome Baroque house standing behind the Tall Pavilion to enjoy and command these sheets of water and soldierly clipped yews. I can

11

just remember the 1895 house which stood there until the 1960s, but its demolition was no architectural loss. In 1902 the current squire, Colchester-Wemyss, was strapped for cash and undertook to tutor the Crown Prince of Siam (present day Thailand) in the subtleties of English country-house parties. The young prince Vajiravudh took to his lessons enthusiastically, particularly the amateur theatricals, writing and producing in the corrugated-iron village hall three short comic sketches, with lavish costumes. The visit was such a success that three of his royal brothers followed him at Westbury and when he became King Vajiravudh he helped his improvident old tutor out financially.

Curiously the original Westbury Court of Maynard Colchester I never really related to the long axis of the garden. It was a quaint Tudor house which, like the present old people's home, stood aside from all this impressive geometry and had its grand front to the churchyard. But now, as you turn back left at the fountain and the little 'yew houses', comes the autumnal climax of the garden: the great West Wall with plums, pears and apples in that order. If you have ever wondered what a seventeenth-century Jargonelle pear looked like, here is the answer – it is monstrous – or Jacobean apples or Tudor fruit? They are all here – history being tunnelled by wasps. Incidentally the National Trust puts a free basket of fruit for you to sample in the viewing room of the Tall Pavilion and I think Calville Rouge d'Hiver of 1600 was the juiciest. Generally they had grudging flavours and, by modern standards, were very dry, but what an experience. So how about a Jacobean vegetable garden for the Trust's next project?

Before you leave Westbury you might want to enjoy the unrestored textures of the church with its Colchester monuments. If you can get the key to the isolated church tower its spire is internally a wonderful forest of fourteenth-century woodwork, Forest of Dean oak. Otherwise the *Red Lion* is close by for good pub food.

In the Steps of a Dead Poet

Prior Park Landscape Garden, Bath

Theme: Prior Park has the two most theatrically beautiful garden vistas anywhere in England. Studley Royal and Stourhead are both richer in features and woodlands but neither have anything as dramatic as the views down to and up from Prior Park's Palladian Bridge. There is not a great deal else to see but the National Trust makes a great play with the relics of Alexander Pope's Rococo layout. Enjoy the park for its elegiac duo of Palladian house and Palladian garden building, but be warned: the paths are steep.

Directions: And here is a problem. Prior Park may be on Bath's doorstep, visible from any number of viewpoints in the city, presiding like some royal residence over a compact principality, but your car is not an easy option. Parking on the steep slopes of Combe Down is virtually impossible, though there are four or five places for the disabled by the ticket kiosk. To encourage you to take a No.2 or 4 bus from the last bus stop in Dorchester Street, between the rail and bus stations, the National Trust cuts £1 off your entrance fee on presentation of a return ticket. So please take the short ride. Buses run every ten minutes and the trip is a pleasure, particularly if you sit on the left-hand side. Prior Park Road has a spanking set of trim late-Regency villas that suddenly end with two Victorian Gothic delights. Then, after John Wood the Elder's Lower Lodge, you will be riding alongside the park with tempting glimpses of the Rock Gate and the deep valley below. The bus will drop you at the entrance gates and the price of the ticket includes a good map of your route.

Opening Times and Entrance Fees: The garden is open daily, except Tuesdays, Christmas Day, Boxing Day and New Year's Day, from 12 noon to 5.30pm; £3.80 for adults, £1.90 for children.

Things to look out for:
1   The 'horrid' wreck of Alexander Pope's 'Wilderness'
2   The Sham Bridge, which hardly looks like a bridge at all
3   An outdoor church intended for Catholic triumphalism
4   Graffiti and the changing writing style of vandals over the
    centuries
5   Woodland Place, a very superior residential terrace
6   Pope's, or Mrs Allen's Grotto

Garden Tour

Be prepared to absorb impacts early on as there is a concentration of interesting, as opposed to beautiful, features on your first level stretch of woodland walk to the right. Ignore the side trip up to the Grotto; it will fit in better at the end. And please do not turn left down the hill; the anti-clockwise circuit to the right is the way to view the landscape. You are already in Alexander Pope's 'Wilderness' or 'Cabinet', an area which it is now fashionable to describe as a 'Rococo Garden' and one which the National Trust, in its eager quest for authenticity, means to recreate. At the moment, Spring 1999, there is very little left of a cluster of garden features – no Serpentine Lake, no Gothick Temple, no statue of Moses striking the rock – so first some useful history.

Prior Park was entirely the creation, between 1735 and 1764, of one formidable entrepreneur, politician and industrial magnate: Ralph Allen, several times mayor of Bath. He became hugely rich by running the postal services for the whole country, building rows of houses in Bath and organising the local stone quarries with a shrewd mix of philanthropy, union bashing and innovations in transport. His house, which is soon going to burst fabulously into view along this path, is ducal in scale, a palace by any European standard, but Allen had no taste for personal grandeur. His tremendous Palladian three-part mansion was built as a sales gimmick, a showroom on a grand scale to sell the stone from his quarries at Combe Down up the hill. Rival quarry owners at Portland had put out the rumour that Bath stone was so soft maggots could breed in it. Prior Park was Allen's answer to them, but it is only a palace of outward show. Its interiors have, even before two devastating fires in 1836 and 1992, always been unimaginative and inferior. Allen and his wife lived in very modest suites of rooms, first in the west wing and then in the east, so you are not missing anything by being excluded from the house, which is now a private school, Catholic and co-educational.

Allen achieved his garden by a process of trial and error, and the poet Alexander Pope was one of those trials and one of those errors. Pope had created, between 1720 and 1730, a clever little garden across the road from his villa at Twickenham and made it nationally famous by his writings. Thereafter he made a habit of scraping up aristocratic acquaintances and going to stay for months on end with tolerant lords to advise them on garden design. He had had his eye on Ralph Allen for several years before he managed an invitation to the newly completed west wing of Prior Park in 1739. That was when Allen, impressed by Pope's reputation and friends, laid out the 'Wilderness' to the poet's bidding. But while closely packed garden features on winding paths in a shrubby wood may have been the right solution for a flat, Thames-side garden, they were quite inappropriate to Allen's grandiose house and this precipitous grassy hillside.

John Wood, Allen's first architect, had sited Prior Park superbly, commanding this deep combe with an entire city posed at the bottom like the ultimate in garden buildings. Grand garden solutions were required, not winding paths with toy events in a shrubbery, but the architect was partly to blame. Wood had conceived the house as three sides of an ideal twelve-sided figure and drawn imaginary lines to a supposed centre point half way down the hill. So instead of including the whole glorious valley into his garden Allen had, with much effort, created an artificial pond at that half-way point and made that the limit of his layout. With vegetable gardens on the far, eastern side of the combe and Pope's winding paths on the west it was an opportunity missed and it is good to learn that the manipulative poet had a miserable time staying with the Allens. He complained of 'Regularity of dining and the Simplicity of the Food, but one Glass [of wine] a day, and four days in six not a drop ... Tho' I enjoy deep Quiet, I can't say I have much Pleasure or even any Object that obliges me to smile'.

A few relics of Pope's Wilderness lie around you in the woodland. There is a Cascade coming down from his ruined Grotto and an excavation to show you the banks of a lost Serpentine Lake; but opening up through the trees beyond a round pond and the puzzling Sham Bridge is the satisfying golden stone confidence of Prior Park mansion. I am not an uncritical enthusiast for Palladian Revival architecture but here it works superbly, looking the very essence of aristocratic good taste even though it was built by 'low born' Allen as a sales pitch. The more confused range of buildings, up on your right behind the trees, are the premises of St Paul's College, now part of the school but converted in 1831 by the Catholic Bishop Baines from Wood's original Doric west wing. It includes a fine neo-Classical chapel. The east wing, visible over the trees, became St Peter's College, a seminary for priests.

The next two hundred yards are sheer landscape magic. On your right the great house stands proudly above green lawns, stone urns and Bishop Baines's tremendous flight of steps designed for open-air Corpus Christi ceremonies. Down to the left is the breathtaking, headlong descent of the combe to the twin lakes and that perfect eye-catcher, the Palladian Bridge. In late autumn when the flanking arms of woodland are ablaze with the turning leaves of beech, chestnut and oak, the valley becomes almost too poetic, like a stage set for grand opera. In full summer you can see that the planting has been, as Pope urged but hardly practised, painterly, with a subtle play of light and medium greens against the dark yews; and from this point above it all you can just make out the site of that first mistaken pond.

Now comes the long descent through open woodland with the sound of unseen waters always in your ears and a tribe of grey squirrels lurking and bouncing behind every other tree trunk. Full marks to the Trust for the path's surface of limestone rubble crushed smooth but not slippery. At the bottom of the hill is Fishponds Cottage and another steep valley coming down from the right, but your dilemma will be whether to take the path between the two lakes or go right round the lower lake before turning back. Either way the views up the hill are idyllic. Now the Palladian Bridge frames the view and Prior Park has become, in its turn, the garden's

eye-catcher with only the main house visible. Allen had sacked John Wood in 1737 when only the basement was built, but he continued to use Wood's design, a cleverly modified version of Colen Campbell's 1717 second version for Wanstead House in Essex.

The Palladian Bridge is another modified copy, this time of Roger Morris's original bridge of 1736-7 over the river Nadder at Wilton House near Salisbury. Allen's clerk of works, Richard Jones, erected this brilliant piece of plagiarism in 1755 and Lord Camelford is usually given the credit for its placing. That may be unfair to Ralph Allen as there is every sign that once he had got rid of Pope he was slowly but deliberately extending his garden downwards to take proper advantage of the existing natural configuration of the valley. Capability Brown came to Prior Park quite late in the development of the grounds and was only paid £60 for a survey and plans which have not survived, but he is likely to have advised on the tree planting and the drainage. If you are a graffiti fan you will enjoy separating the true antiques on the columns of the bridge from those of twentieth-century schoolboys. 'Dowling', 'Slater' and 'WWL' are my favourites for their eighteenth-century calligraphy.

The long climb back up the hill has one incident, the Rock or Chinese Gate, recently recreated by the Trust with chunks of tufa dredged out of the lakes. The only other carrot I can offer on this stretch is a view across the valley to Woodland Place up on the skyline. This is the most enviable terrace in Bath as its residents are automatically guardians and owners of a private wood up that side valley. When you have panted your way back to the entrance kiosk, duty should compel you to walk the extra few yards to the hideous ruin of Pope's grotto, enclosed within a corrugated-iron shed. Mrs Allen buried the corpse of a Great Dane puppy which Pope had given her as a thank-you present for all those glasses of wine. Apparently it did not live very long so Pope composed an epitaph for it:

> Weep not,
> Tread lightly my grave,
> Call me Pet.

Hardly an inspired offering for the poor dog and also rather mysterious as it was not called 'Pet' at all, but 'Miss Bounce'. A floor of ammonites arranged like the rays of the sun awaits the Trust's restoration. The bus stop for your return is 70 yards up the road.

Arcadia Achieved

Stourhead Landscape, Wiltshire

Theme: The seventeenth-century French artist, Claude Lorrain, painted ideal landscapes of classical temples set among great trees and idyllic waters. In the eighteenth century a retired banker, Henry Hoare, set about realising Claude's vision in a Wiltshire valley where the river Stour rises from six wells. For me this is not just the most eventful garden in England, but a time-trip back into mid-Georgian aesthetic values.

Directions: Stourton village lies on a narrow lane west of the B3092 between Frome in Somerset and Mere in Wiltshire. If you are driving there on a fine weekend you will know you are getting close when you see ridges of bare green downland and the sky alive with paragliders. As you approach the house you will see a sign for a right turn to Alfred's Tower, one of Stourhead's outlying architectural features. Follow the signs for a mile or two if you want to see the Tower before you visit the garden. Then return to the main road, pass the front of the house and turn right to Stourton village, then left into the car-park where you buy your tickets for the garden and also, if you take my advice, for Stourhead House, in that low barn where typical National Trust representatives are waiting to greet you with effusive gentility.

Opening Times and Entrance Fees: The Garden is open daily all the year from 9am-7pm or dusk if that is earlier; the house is open from 27 March to 31 October, Saturdays to Wednesdays, 12-5.30pm, or dusk if earlier. Teas with fabulous fudge cake are served in the Garden Centre while the *Spread Eagle* serves lunches, teas and refreshments. Admission to the Garden is usually £4.50, children £2.50, family £10.00 but from November to the end of February it is £3.50, children £1.50, family £8.00. A combined house and garden ticket costs £8.00, children £3.80, family £20.00 – a stiff price but worth every pound.

Things to look out for:
1   The Roman poet Virgil's directions to the Underworld
2   A cathedral of beech trees
3   St Peter's Pump
4   A Convent in the Woods, but I have never managed to find it
5   A Classical temple which has gone Baroque
6   Lots of stunning nude statues

Garden Tour:

If you are visiting Stourhead between Easter and November you will have to make a choice as between those dates you can either approach the garden as Henry Hoare intended you to, directly from the house, taking in a series of carefully prepared and astonishingly beautiful viewpoints, or you can enter through the common visitor's gate in the village. If you take this last way you will see some of Stourhead's most exciting features straight away instead of keeping them as a climax at the end of your circuit.

Let us suppose you are a summer visitor. From the ticket barn follow the winding path down through the trees, cross the lane by the footbridge and reach the house drive via the kitchen gardens. The way down into the valley is clearly marked and branches off to the left by a second ticket kiosk. But let me recommend a visit to the house first for two reasons. Its rooms are literally crammed with paintings that explain what the Hoares were aiming at in the garden – wild Italian landscapes, views of temples and watercolours of the actual garden at various stages in its construction. Spend a thoughtful hour in those rooms and you too can become a garden historian! The second reason is the Library. When the afternoon sun streams into it that is one of the ten most perfect rooms in Britain.

Back on the gentry route down into the garden keep looking out for carefully prepared gaps in the trees. These are all planned to give you picturesque thrills in eighteenth-century terms. The first one on the left frames the village church tower. Then, if you are alert, you will see a little stone marker inscribed: '1 View Point to the Obelisk', but not a sign of an obelisk. Be patient; the trees have grown up a little too much. If you turn off right on that level path for about twenty yards you will be rewarded with one of the three best vistas in Stourhead – an avenue of lean, tall silvery beech trees offering an attenuated frame for the needle-sharp Obelisk of the Sun, first raised in 1746 as an eyecatcher from the house, but infinitely more moving seen here in an apparent forest.

Retrace your steps and continue zig-zagging gently downwards. The Temple of Apollo shows up briefly to the left ambushed in trees and pure Claude in its composition. Glimmers of water and glimpses, possibly not intended at this point, of the Pantheon will lead you on down to another marker: 'The Lake and the Grotto' where again the trees have grown up and you will only see what you are meant to see in winter. Don't turn right here or you will miss the Temple of Flora. Go straight ahead until you join the common visitor's circumambulating route around the lake. Turn right and enjoy a few winding yards of sensationally composed lake views with the Pantheon's dome and the sinister Grotto cave across the waters. Henry Hoare did think of building a mosque with a minaret on one island but never managed it. That path which you have just descended once had a Venetian Seat, a Turkish Tent and one, or even two, Chinese pavilions to divert visitors. Henry was a great eclectic builder with a child-like delight in fantasy features. His grandson, Richard Colt Hoare, who took over Stourhead on Henry's death in 1785, was a more reserved and scholarly classicist. He appreciated his grandfather's interest in Virgil and Aeneas but swept away most of the exotic seats and pavilions. So what you see now is a 1746-85 layout as tidied up by a neo-Classicist between 1785 and 1838, when Colt Hoare died aged eighty.

As you reach the temple of Flora (originally dedicated to Ceres) you must come to grips with Virgil's poem, the *Aeneid*, but enjoy the Temple's Tuscan severity first and its marvellously chaste interior. Henry Flitcroft designed it and a local builder, William Privet, built the Temple in 1744-6. The Coade stone copy of the Borghese Vase was made in 1772 and originally stood in that lost Venetian Seat up the hill. In his wanderings after the fall of Troy, Aeneas had to consult the Cumaean Sybil before he descended into the Underworld to be told to found Rome, so the Sybil warned him, 'Procul, O procul este profani' ('Begone, you who are uninitiated! Begone!') which words you will find carved over the door of the Temple.

Walk on around the lake. You will not see much of it because the National Trust has, wisely I think, set the path back from the shore in order to preserve the lake's idyllic isolation, and the trees themselves screen the views, with azaleas and rhododendrons in Spring, which are a pleasure. The Trust sells a guide: *Mature Trees in the Stourhead Landscape*. When the path turns into an isthmus-walk, between the lake and a large pond, you will come, as quite often in Stourhead, to choices. If you turn off right before the isthmus path begins, then a long pleasant walk of more than half a mile up the valley of Six Wells Bottom will bring you to one of Henry Hoare's exotic collection which grandson Richard never bothered to demolish. This is St Peter's Pump, a pretty Renaissance structure rescued by Henry from St Peter's Street, Bristol in 1766. If you want to save your legs, wait until the other side of the isthmus, turn right fifty yards up to a huge redwood and there, with no further effort, you will see the Pump perched on its rocky grotto base, far away up the valley.

Back on the circular walk and the next choice is a moral one, or so the Aeneas theorists claim. As the path forks you can either go virtuously right, on a direct route to the Gothic Cottage and the wholesome Pantheon, the Temple of Hercules, or you can dip down left through a very gloomy planting of laurel, holly, yew and ilex into the dangers of the Underworld. Turn left is my advice or you will miss Stourhead's greatest thrill, the Grotto of the Nymphs. As the dark trees close in you will face an unlit tunnel of jagged rocks. The sound of falling water leads on into a dimly lit vaulted space. To the right a nymph sleeps over a waterfall and there is a plunge pool, for naked bathing in the eighteenth century, but not now. Straight ahead a leaden, yet oddly life-like statue of a river god beckons to you from another gloomy vault and to your left, perfectly framed by rocks, is Stourton village church and the Bristol High Cross. Henry Hoare, two hundred years dead, has trapped you in an extraordinary triple image of picturesque aesthetics. Relish it for you will never experience one more vivid.

The River God, modelled by John Cheere on a Salvator Rosa engraving of Aeneas and Father Tiber, is pointing the way out of this Kingdom of the Dead to the temple of healthy Hercules, so climb the steps back up into daylight, enjoy the Gothic Cottage, which has a seat commanding views across to Flora and a rocky boathouse, and come to Hercules in that Pantheon which has centred so many lake views in the windings of the path.

Flitcroft built this in 1753-4, or so the authorities claim, but when Bishop Pococke came here in 1754 he only saw an open round Ionic temple. If the Pantheon's door is unlocked another time trip can be taken. The interior is solemn, more holy temple than sculpture gallery. Hercules carved by Michael Rysbrack after 1756 stands massively nude in a low terracotta light. This, one feels, is what pagan awe might really have felt like. Personally I could do without the other statues – Flora, Diana, St Susanna (after Henry's daughter), Ceres, Meleager and Isis. They detract a little from the presiding Hercules. Originally there was a heating system though how Henry used it as a study and could have read in this dim light is a puzzle. Venus Callipygos in lead on the outside of the Pantheon is a reminder of how sexy the classics could be.

On over a graceful iron bridge of 1860 where a drive to the right should lead to a Convent in the Woods. I have tried three times to reach it and failed, but as it is a private house that is probably how the Trust would prefer it – an unattainable mystery in the trees. More elegant lake vistas, a cascade tumbling down to the right and you are walking on a great earth dam of 1754 which made the lake possible. One last side trip has to be made unless you are tired out. Turn right up a rockwork bridge over a public road, pass the slight relics of a rocky Hermitage and you will come out on a green plateau, the Walk of the Muses, where the Temple of Apollo over-looks the entire lake basin with all its garden buildings. If you ever thought of classical architecture as pure and simple this temple is an eye-opener. Based on a temple at Baalbek in Lebanon its Corinthian columns and semi-circular niches perform a stately waltz about the central dome. When Flitcroft finished this in 1765, the same year that the Bristol High Cross was erected on the level ground below it, Stourhead was virtually complete.

Stagger back to the main path, take in the charming Palladian Bridge of 1762 and the High Cross itself, which Bristol foolishly gave away in 1764, then enter the parish church to pay your respects to Henry Hoare who made this poetic, leafy Arcadia out of bare downland

slopes. His monument is over on the south aisle wall and the marble scroll above the regular funerary details says it all in ringing couplets:

> With grateful Reverence to this marble lean
> Rais'd to the Friendly Founder of the Scene.
> Here with pure love of smiling Nature warm'd.
> This far famed Demy-Paradise he form'd.
> And happier still from Heaven he learn'd to find
> A sweeter Eden in a bounteous mind.
> Thankful those fair and flowery paths he trod
> And priz'd them only as they lead to God.

A Sleeping Garden of Pan
that woke up just in time

Painswick Rococo Garden, Gloucestershire

Theme: A hidden Cotswold valley where a typical bourgeois layout of the 1740s dreamed on for 230 years, its extraordinary concentration of Gothick and Classical buildings, miniature vistas, clear pools and trickling rivulets slowly decaying and becoming overgrown, but surviving when all its contemporary gardens were lost or transformed. Then in 1984, when conifers and nettles had almost taken over, Lord and Lady Dickinson, with a devoted committee of experts, began a process of restoration and rebuilding so that now Painswick Rococo Garden is recognisable as the place which Thomas Robins painted with loving precision in 1748.

Directions: From Bath take the scenic A46 along the high Cotswolds. From Nailsworth onwards through Stroud to Painswick you will see evidence everywhere of the region's lost prosperity, woollen mills and handsome mill owners' houses. As you approach Painswick the limestone takes on a pure silvery quality. Don't let the architecture in the little town distract you from a sharp left turn in the centre then up the hill with Painswick House, or 'Buenos Aires' as it was known when Thomas Robins painted it, on your left as soon as you leave the houses. The only sign of the garden will be a strange pigeon house away across the park, all the other surprises are hidden.

Opening Times and Entrance Fees: The Garden is open from the second Wednesday in January to 30 November, 11am-5pm, Wednesday to Sunday inclusive (plus Bank Holidays); daily during July and August. Coffee, lunches and teas are served in the licensed Coach House Restaurant. £3 for adults, £2.70 for senior citizens, £1.60 for children aged 6-16, for whom Painswick makes a particular provision with treasure and nature trails changing every year. They sell a family ticket for £8.00.

Things to look out for:
1   Hints of an eighteenth-century Pan cult
2   A brand new maze opening in 1999
3   Two stars within hexagons – one old, one new
4   An eighteenth-century Cold Bath that actually looks tempting
5   A garden building designed to squint
6   The artist painting the original garden

Garden Tour:

To get the unique flavour of this garden I would suggest a coffee first in the Coach House. This will give you time to take in the highly complex details of that Thomas Robins painting which you will find reproduced on the guide book, posters and postcards. The real excitement of this garden is that we have this meticulous visual record of its first condition and that so much has survived or been accurately restored. Keep away from the Coach House's famous treacle tart. That is a treat to reserve for later.

Now off under the arch and through the Melon Ground. Walled and enclosed with roses, hollyhocks, clematis, fig trees and southernwood, this seems to be preparing you for a conventional flower garden but then, through the second arch, comes the *coup d'oeil*. The ground drops away and all the complexities of the hidden valley are laid out before you, very nearly exactly as it was when Benjamin Hyett, a fairly wealthy Gloucester lawyer, finished planting it in the late 1740s. His father Charles had built the house, Buenos Aires as he called it, then Benjamin, a leading figure in a local gentleman's club dedicated to drinking, midnight revelry and Pan worship, created the garden as a secret place for high jinks and naughty goings-on. We refer to it now as a 'Rococo Garden' which would suggest a place of curls and winding intricacies but, as you can already see from this lofty viewpoint, most of the garden's little vistas are ruler-straight or geometrical like the diamond-shaped Kitchen Garden which you see below you. The Dickinsons together with Lady Dickinson's son, Paul Moir, have wisely taken the plunge and restored the vegetables to the prominence the eighteenth century would have given them – National Trust take note and return the vegetable enclosure to Westbury Court's water garden.

Left or right-hand turns are equally attractive at this point. Either way will lead to a complete circumnavigation and, as I like to keep the best to the last, let us turn left for the Eagle House which stands all pink and new at the same level as where you are standing. Robins admired this saucy garden house so much that he painted a separate picture of it, poised above its grotto. With the help of archaeologists, who discovered that the room was an extruded hexagon in shape, an accurate rebuilding has been possible. But the grotto, down the steep, winding path, is original, half Classical niches, half Gothick arch, the embodiment of that stylistically confused period.

Watch your footing and continue downhill to the Bowling Green with the diamond of the Kitchen Garden pointing back up the hill to the white curve of the Exedra and that marvellous clump of towering beech trees which makes all the other features of the garden look frail and toy-like. But the Exedra is for later.

Walk on with trees and the house up to your left and the Fish Pond with its Pergola walk to your right. Take the Pergola in now as it is a restored Robins feature and you will not be passing under it unless you want a short cut and are ready to miss some of the garden's most enjoyable outer reaches. A sign will direct you up and left to the Beech Walk. This is a second, if minor surprise: a long straight walk between young beeches with a three-arched Gothick Alcove at the end. Robins illustrated this as a Classical building, which is puzzling, but Benjamin Hyett seems to have favoured Gothick for its haunted associations.

At the Alcove another path points up left to the Pigeon House. This is a *cul-de-sac* and you will be returning by the same route, but the short digression is well worth taking. On the way to the Pigeon House you have views down right to a pond with an island and left to Painswick House itself. Only the middle five bays are Charles Hyett's work – an attractive fusion of Baroque and Palladian details – the wings are Regency additions. Now comes one of the garden's mysteries. Is the Pigeon House meant to symbolise something obscure? Circles, octagons and squares are all involved in its features, the upstairs room affords no garden view and the downstairs room has a strange, possibly cabalistic, floor: a six-pointed star within a hexagon. The building predates the garden and you will see the artist sitting by it sketching the garden layout in his painting.

Back at the Gothick Alcove take the path down behind the little building and you will find yourself in the Wilderness. There was once a Hermit's Cell here and the Rococo Garden Trust intends to restore it to its Robins appearance. As you bend back up the valley a small stepped rill comes down on your left with a rockery, a very Rococo feature. Back at the other end of the Pergola you begin quite a steep climb but one with distractions to the right and constantly changing vistas across and down this complex area. At one corner of the Fish Pond is the Hydraulic Ram House which supplied Painswick House with its water until 1955. Then don't miss the side trip (signed) to the Plunge Pool, or more properly, the Cold Bath. This was a focus for Benjamin and his merry men, a place where they could strip off, leap into the crystal clear water and pay their respects to the great god Pan whose sinister, highly threatening statue by Van Nost once stood beside the pool (see the Robins painting). Such statues are vulnerable to vandals and thieves so Pan has been moved into the hall of Painswick House, though I would find it spooky living with the wood god in my house. Painswick had a bad reputation in the eighteenth century for drunken riots and debauchery surrounding a pagan Pan festival.

Up along a beautiful hedge of variegated beech past the Doric Seat you come to another side trip, up left to inspect the maze and, if you wish, to climb to the viewpoint with its seat. I prefer to stress the enclosed character of the garden so I skip this admittedly fine vantage point. The Robins painting is somewhat vague at this area. His Exedra is, however, sharply illustrated and this has enabled the Trust to recreate it from scratch with yet another pool in this abundantly watered combe. Below the Exedra is a pleasant rope garden, full of sweet-scented herbs and fragrant with jasmine in the Summer. I can never resist a vegetable garden and find the display of giant rhubarb, leeks and cabbages handsome enough in a homely way. Thinking I was learning about old varieties of apples I began taking down their names from the metal plaques until I noticed one reading 'In Loving Memory of .....' and realised that these were the names of donors, patrons of the garden, a body of people which you can join if you wish on your return to the Coach House and that treacle tart. The scarecrow is no substitute for Pan, rabbits rather than birds are the chief predators of the garden.

If you are looking for an appropriately curvaceous Rococo path after all these straight lines of espaliers and yew hedges then the next stretch up alongside the splendid stand of beech trees is authentically Rococo and 'artinatural', as the eighteenth century liked to call such configurations. Rococo is an early nineteenth-century composite invention from two French words, *rocaille* (rocky) and *coquille* (shells). Ahead of you is the jewel of the garden, the Red House. This carefully detailed double garden house survived the long decline intact and only needed its new coat of red limewash. Eighteenth-century garden buildings were often painted in this extrovert style and it is the cheeky, colourful air of the garden which makes Painswick so authentic. That mellow air of weathered limestone which we tend to associate with gardens of the period such as Stourhead is not authentic at all but just something which time and purist later owners have brought about. Stourhead was once crowded like Painswick with cheerful painted features like the Red House.

The interior is surprisingly cosy. One neat little parlour has a fireplace and the Hyetts' arms with their motto in plaster above it. '*Cor immobile*' means 'a constant heart'. A most enjoyable and very rare feature is the asymmetry of the two rooms which enables them to command two quite separate vistas. Compare the Red House with the Eagle House (which should have been painted the same deep satisfying red) and I think you will agree that a competent architect designed one and a complete amateur the other, but that is all part of the garden's essential contrary charm. Take in the relatively long main axis of the garden down to the Bowling Green, another feature I would love to activate for either gentle bowling or spiteful croquet, and then one straight walk will bring you back to the arch and the Melon Ground, not forgetting the treacle tart.

If you have time for a leisurely return and a search for the Pan cult of Painswick (Pan's Wyck as Robins calls it on some of his paintings for Hyett) find Beacon House on the main street, overlooking the churchyard. This is where the gentry of the Pan cult held their ceremonial dinners under a ceiling decorated with a remarkable image in plaster of the Lycian Apollo, protector of shepherds and their flocks and where Pan with his pipes peers out from the plasterwork. Pan's Lodge where midnight revelries were held has been demolished long ago; it was built by Hyett in the woods on the other side of the valley. One other relic has survived but you will have to thread a tangle of steep valley lanes below the little town to find it, and this is the stables where the Pan fans used to leave their carriages before walking up to the Lodge. It is a strange tall structure, originally painted red like the garden buildings but now converted into a desirable residence for one of Painswick's genteel population. Don't expect the present town to nurture even the remotest whiff of diabolical activities. There was another small statue of Pan in the churchyard of all places, but back in the 1950s the vicar had it discretely buried and I suspect that they have even forgotten where it was entombed. Just as well!

A Carriage-ride to the
Castle Perilous

Blaise Castle Estate, Henbury, Bristol

Theme: An authentic Jane Austen experience: these are the Picturesque pleasure grounds with cliffs, hanging woods and Gothick castle that Catherine Morland was planning to visit in the novelist's *Northanger Abbey* on that disastrous day when Catherine inadvertently left Henry Tilney standing. In actual fact she never got to Blaise, but if you navigate your way through Bristol you will not only have the scenic carriage-drive that Humphry Repton planned, but the Hamlet, nine cottages of excruciating charm, designed in 1811, as if for full-sized gnomes, by John Nash to stand around an orchard green – an intact scrap of Regency England.

Directions: Be brave. You must cross Bristol making for the A4018, signposted for Westbury-on-Trym. After crossing the Downs, which are green, open and unmissable, your road dips downhill. Drive through the suburban housing of Westbury and turn left, at the fourth set of traffic lights where Blaise Castle is signposted, up Henbury Road. As soon as you reach the top of this wooded hill and begin to drop downwards, signal left and park in a comfortable widening of the road in front of a scatter of houses. You have just passed the entrance to the Estate so walk back up and take the first narrow drive on your right. Up in the dark trees is a handsome Gothic lodge, Repton's first mood setter. You are on your way.

Opening Times and Entrance Fees: The Estate is open daily all year round, but the gate at this top entrance is locked each evening at 5.15 pm. Blaise Castle Museum is open from 3 April to late Autumn: Tuesday to Sunday, 10am-1pm and 2pm-5pm; admission is free.

Things to look out for:

1   The grooves Repton's men drilled for gunpowder when
    blasting rocks
2   Timber Lodge, a mysterious bark house which could be
    1750 or 1815 – decide!
3   A clover-leaf folly tower, not as easy to spot as you might
    expect
4   The definitive Grecian urn
5   England's first garden suburb
6   Scipio's grave

Garden Tour:

Repton's sales technique was to write and illustrate one-off
'Red Books' – a bound volume in Moroccan leather – and give it
to a park owner. By a series of overlapping flaps, showing before
and after scenes, this would suggest what improvements could be
achieved by careful planting and building if the owner was prepared
to pay a small fortune. In 1796 the wealthy Quaker banker, John
Scandrett Harford, fell for this ploy. He was having a new classical
house built on the edge of Henbury village, but the grounds he had
bought included a suprisingly wild area of hills and ravines where
an earlier landowner, Thomas Farr, had, in 1766, built an impressive
Gothick folly tower. This is Blaise Castle and it explains why
Harford's Classical house should have such an inappropriate name
– Blaise Castle House. The hills were already a favourite picnic
spot for Bristolians and Mr Harford with Quaker good will,
decided to let Repton loose on the area and plan a scenic carriage-
ride. This lodge then was built, not to mark a route in to the house,
but as the start of a Gothic experience with a thrill every few hundred
yards, provided you were a delicate soul with a Picturesque
sensibility and prepared to enter into the spirit of Gothic novels
like *The Monk* or *The Mysteries of Udolpho*.

In that spirit pass under the arch of the lodge and study the
excellent map on the notice board. Now holly, yews and ilexes
close in to make you apprehensive and the drive, which can be
muddy so wear sensible shoes, winds into the woods to bring you
to the mystery house, the Timber Lodge. Someone designed this

as a perfect *des. res.* for the local witch. It looks like a park feature of about 1750, but it is not shown on Repton's map and it is in such good condition that I incline to a date of about 1815 or thereabouts. John Nash's cottages in the Hamlet, which you will be seeing soon, have very much the same roofs and they are of 1811. Make your own mind up and press on to an authentic Repton feature, the Woodman's Cottage. He was proud of this. It once had a covered veranda where you could rest. 'The idea to be excited', Repton wrote, 'was "la Simplicité soignée" '. Remember that the grounds already had an earlier Gothick folly castle. In 1795 it was important for a landscape to have painterly qualities and Repton claimed that smoke from this cottage chimney would 'spread a thin veil along the glen, and produce that kind of vapoury repose over the opposite wood which painters often attempt to describe'. He was, you will notice, a born salesman.

Zig-zag back down the ravine. Here the drive (have you seen any gunpowder grooves?) is meant to 'excite admiration and surprize, without any mixture of that terror which, tho' partaking of the sublime, is very apt to destroy the delights of romantic scenery'. Indeed it has been very carefully and expensively engineered to give carriages an even ride.

Stratford Mill was here before Repton's time. He ignored it because it didn't fit into the Picturesque, so we had better do the same. Cross the little Hazel Brook. Our route lies up to the right but, if you feel like a side trip, the track to the left leads on to the Giant's Soap Dish, a formation in the stream, and the Lily Pond. You will, however, have to return by the same way. My advice is to take the right-hand drive and then just as the woods are ending take the signposted path up to your left. This will take you higher and higher up above the ravine with 'admiration and surprize' being excited at every turn. The steepest, sheerest section of wooded cliff is called Lover's Leap for obvious reasons. And then, more surprize and admiration as the woods suddenly open out into a broad green meadow with Blaise Castle in the middle of it, looking for all the world like one of those enchanter's towers in the Arthurian legends. In Summer the tower is open and you can climb up to enjoy the view, otherwise, though you are on a hill top there is no view at all; you are enclosed in this green mock mediaeval world of woodland. It is a most curious experience and well worth the climb.

Now take the broad drive down through the trees; here again there could be side trips to the left to see the Butcher's Cave and the Robber's Cave. Let me just warn you that neither of them go very deep and Mr Harford's house down the drive is much more interesting. You will see it ahead of you as you break out of the trees into an open green space where the Gothic atmosphere fades right away. The house was built for Harford by William Paty, a Bristol architect of only modest talents, but the Orangery curving away to the right is a John Nash addition. Walk along it past the huge holm oak and you will come to a secret garden between the house and Henbury village church with a charming (the word has to be used heavily for the rest of this visit) thatched Dairy, again by Nash.

Retrace your steps to enjoy the circular Ionic porch to the house, the Grecian urn and the gate posts with horses' heads. These lead past the stables to the road. At this point you really must be firm and make the detour, a mere 250 yards, to Blaise Hamlet, there is nothing else in Britain quite like it. So turn left into Henbury Road, enjoy the two trim Regency villas, then turn right down Hallen Road for the last 150 yards and on the left, very easily missed, is a little opening in the wall leading into the Hamlet.

Frankly I find it sheer enchantment. Nine cottages, each one designed like a different ornament to put on a mantelpiece. Some are thatched, some tiled, some Cotswold slated. Two have pigeon cotes built in and every one is ingeniously bowed and nooked and sheltered by eaves and covings. Take your time here to absorb the detail and the detachment of it all from the real world – no street lights, no car access, no tarmac paths. Every cottage has outside seats to encourage sociability and community feeling; it was here that the idea of garden villages like Port Sunlight and Bournville was first put in the public mind. So spare a grateful thought for John Scandrett Harford who not only made his grounds into a pleasure place for the middle class, but created the Hamlet as a perfect almshouse for his elderly servants. The stone dial and parish pump, artfully off-centre in the green, has an inscription by Harford's son.

Now make your way back to the stables gate and turn down quiet Church Lane; take a right turning at the pretty Tudor-style village hall of 1830, a sure sign of wealthy local residents, and you will be in the churchyard. Naturally the church is locked, but you are here on a politically correct pilgrimage to the grave of Scipio Africanus. This is on the right of the path to the church porch and easily picked out as its cherub heads have been blackwashed. Poor Scipio died when he was only 18 and the lines on his stone claim:

> I who was born a pagan and a slave
> Now sweetly sleep a Christian in my grave.

Which tends to make Bristol people feel guilty about their involvement in the Slave Trade. But there were never slaves in Bristol because legally they automatically became free as soon as they stepped off a boat onto British soil.

When you have paid your respects you might notice the coping of the entire churchyard wall. This is the longest stretch I know of those specially moulded blocks of black slag from the local brass foundries. There were a few blocks in the walls by Harford's stables; Bristolians liked them for their iridescent qualities in glancing sunlight. Take the path down the churchyard past the east end, with its Victorian versions of Early English lancet windows, and turn into Rectory Gardens. On your left over the wall is Henbury's original manor house, the Henbury Awdlet. Built later than you might guess, in 1675-80, it has tended to be overwhelmed by the number of eighteenth-century merchants' villas set in this desirable fold of the hills. At the end of Rectory Gardens, across the main road, is a curious green wasteland. Here were the formal gardens of the Great House, a barracks of a place, set most unwisely on the corner where two roads met. It is hard to envisage now but originally a straight avenue of trees led from the Great House across the field and up the hill to focus on the exact place where the Blaise Castle folly tower now stands. Jan Kip drew his aerial views of both the Awdlet and the Great House.

Here at last is a pub, *The Salutation*, where you can rest, refresh yourself and think how unsympathetically the place has been extended to damage the containment of the village street. On your way again, uphill back to the car, there are just two more points of interest. Where Trymwood Close branches off the main road, scan the horizon and you should be able to make out another Gothic folly. This was the west window of the Lord Mayor's Chapel on Bristol's College Green, brought out here after a nineteenth-century restoration. Finally, after so much Gothicity, you might find the sturdy Baroque of Chesterfield House a relief. It was probably designed by George Tully who created Dowry Square in the Bristol Hotwells. That ramped parapet is a sure sign of his work. When that went up, around 1730, there was no notion of anything Gothick in the building world, this was a last note of confident classicism and brings you back soberly to your car.

The Vicar, the Gypsy Girl and a Walk into the Underworld

Stancombe Park, Dursley

Theme: Two gardens, one modern with walks and flower borders on a hillside, the other an early nineteenth-century layout hidden below in a secret combe like a stage set for a pastoral opera by Debussy. The modern garden is a reconstruction of an Edwardian enclosure, while legend has it that the valley landscape was created by a vicar with antiquarian interests and an illicit lover.

Directions: Stancombe is just off the B4060 Wotton-under-Edge to Stinchcombe road, about 1¹/₂ miles south-west of Dursley. If you approach it from North Nibley, *The Black Horse* in the village is handy for good pub food. Turn off the B4060 by the little green signposted 'Stancombe/Waterley Bottoms', go past the plain Regency lodge and follow the estate wall until you see the sign for the car-park on your left. Walk back to the rear, courtyard entrance of the house.

Opening Times and Entrance Fees: You will need to organise a group of friends to get into Stancombe as Gerda Barlow conducts tours of the landscape on her own and cannot handle individual visitors. But do try and make up a party as this is a rare experience. The garden is open by appointment, from late April to September. You must write to Mrs Gerda Barlow, Stancombe Park, Stancombe, Dursley, Glos. GL11 6AU; £3 for the garden and £3 for an Austrian tea.

Things to look out for:
1   Roman mosaic panels which introduce a theme of both gardens
2   Cerberus, the guard dog of the Underworld
3   An Egyptian courtyard
4   The bones of a stranded Whale
5   Cornelius, 'Il Porcellino'
6   The Temple of Love

Garden Tour:

As you walk to the back entrance you will see a cast iron weighbridge in the drive stamped 'Bartlett & Son Bristol' and in the bowed wall its mechanism survives behind a wooden door. It has the feel of Brunel's industrial style and sets us firmly in the early nineteenth century. The Purnells were wealthy mill owners in the wool-rich Cotswolds. The original house at Stancombe is in the valley below the present house, which was built by Bransby Purnell sometime between 1811 and 1819 on a new site above the combe to command the spectacular views.

The courtyard is where the owner, Gerda Barlow, serves her delicious Austrian teas to groups of visitors. She has lived at Stancombe for over thirty years and the upper garden is her creation. On the wall under the gilded gryphon, rescued from the Guildhall in London after the bombing, are panels of Roman mosaic, relics from two Roman villas which were discovered in the valley in 1819. It is the Roman history of the area which seems to have given Bransby Purnell the major theme for his secret garden.

On the hillside opposite the house to the west Mrs Barlow has also been inspired by the villas and has had the mosaic designs copied for the top terrace in the upper garden. Set within nineteenth-century parkland of mature Cedars of Lebanon and sweet chestnuts, there is a formal walk with patterned borders of shaped yew and box in the Baroque style. The evergreen framework supports a range of plants chosen specifically for their colour as the seasons change. I saw it recently in Summer with drifts of delicate greens and splashes of deep red from fuschias. To the side is a circular enclosure of trees with a great Italian urn bought from the garden collection of Sir Francis Cooke and this leads to the old rose garden with its Chinoiserie fences, pleached lime walk and seat surrounded by cherubs.

The second garden, always referred to as the 'Folly Garden', is reached by a narrow path which skirts the hillside and drops down to the valley below. On this walk, bordered by shrub roses and comfrey, there are several topiary animals so it has been renamed the Menagerie Walk. As you drop down, your eye follows the chain of ponds in the valley and there are tantalising glimpses

in the distance of the roofs of pavilions with mature trees and shrubs surrounding them. The first sign of the unusual is a small circular enclosure with a font and another mosaic panel set above it. Then the stepping-stone walk winds through a ferny area with huge, almost tropical gunnera leaves dripping water. Soon it becomes a narrow, paved path with deep brick sides, like a sunken pedestrian railway with water rushing underneath the flagstones.

Gunnera leaves part and ahead is a brick wall with a gloomy tunnel entrance. Inside it is pitch dark, but as you become accustomed to the light you are suddenly surprised by a huge stone dog guarding the tunnel. Could this be Cerberus, the dog who guarded the Underworld, and is the whole layout of the Folly Garden inspired by Classical mythology? The bog garden could be the Grove of Persephone which had to be crossed before the Gate of Hades was reached and, unless you were Hercules, Cerberus had to be tamed with cakes and honey; only then could you explore the rivers of Hades. The most famous of these was the Styx and on the other side of it was the Elysian Fields. At Stancombe the tunnel divides into two, go to the right and this opens out into the light and you are on the lakeside (the Styx) with views across the water to the Doric Temple on the other side (the Elysian Fields). The scene here is just like a stage set from Debussy's *Pelléas et Mélisande*.

Next the sunken pathway dives into another tunnel in which there is a fossil collection set in a niche decorated with oyster shells. Out into the open air again the path is flanked by acers and leads to the Egyptian Court. This has three entrances: one to the left gives access to the lake and a landing stage where a boat would take visitors to the Doric Temple (or where Charon would ferry souls across the Styx to the Elysian Fields); the archway to the right, leading originally to an icehouse, is framed by the jaw bone of a whale which got stranded in the Severn, and in front is a curious keyhole opening which leads through another tunnel to a clipped box hedge walk. This lines the southernmost perimeter of the garden and, if you are tall enough, there are views back across the lake and up the valley. Here there is a cast of a wild boar, taken from the bronze statue of 'Il Porcellino' in the Uffizi gallery in Florence; the family call him Cornelius.

At the top of the box walk look back and you will see the tower of North Nibley church on the distant hillside, consciously framed by planting, and then you reach the gardener's cottage. This was once used as a studio by the ladies of nearby Frampton Court who painted the exquisite Frampton flora. Set in the ground are more whale bones – the vertebrae this time – and you approach the Temple with the boathouse below and wide views across the whole layout. The building has a strange façade to the lake which invites entry through recessed sections, but there are no doors, the entrance is hidden away to the side. This deviousness might hint at the practical, as opposed to intellectual, nature of the garden. Local legend has it that the Rev. David Purnell-Edwards, who had married a stout Miss Purnell, built the garden with very narrow entrances so that his wife should not disturb his love-making sessions with a young gypsy girl.

The Doric Temple with its sybaritic new interior, designed by Mrs Barlow's son, Nic, is not open to the public. So walk past the Temple and the flagstone path will lead you to a walled clearing with two pagoda-roofed greenhouses still with their original leaded glazing, wooden seats and shelves for exotics. One has a fountain in the centre and the clearing has as its focus a fountain of swans, both fed originally from an elaborate water system which has dried up. From here you retrace your steps to the lake below the Temple and walk towards the entrance tunnel through an arched pergola. This leads to Cerberus and then to the steep walk back up the valley and your Austrian tea.

Although local legend is often close to fact, no-one is quite sure when the garden was laid out. Some experts have said it dates from the 1840s as it has elements in common with another Folly Garden, that at Biddulph Grange in Staffordshire. However, it is far more likely to have been built by Bransby Purnell after he had finished rebuilding the house. He may well have constructed the garden after the wars with France when soldiers returning from battle were in need of employment and the Egyptian references could be to Napoleon's Nile campaign. Bransby Purnell may have had Stourhead and its Virgilian theme in mind, that would be the intellectual interpretation of the garden's underlying theme. Whereas local folklore would argue a more romantic view, that of the clergyman and his love trysts with a dark-eyed Romany mistress. The languid, Lotos-Eaters atmosphere of the place reminds me of Tennyson's poetry – sorrowing Oenone's many-fountain'd valley of Ida, and a lake for the Lady of Shalott, robed in snowy white, to drift across in her boat.

An Italianate Hill Garden in Wiltshire

Iford Manor, Bradford-on-Avon

Theme: An Edwardian 'Architectural Garden' where the buildings, statuary and sculpture are as important in providing the aesthetic appeal as the planting. It was laid out after 1899 by the Arts and Crafts architect, Harold Ainsworth Peto, with fascinating *objets trouvés* picked up on his travels in Italy.

Directions: The most dramatic way to approach Iford is from the A36 Bath to Warminster road. Take the left turn at a small cross-roads with the Hinton Charterhouse road to your right and drive carefully down the narrow lane to the house and garden by its stream.

Opening Times and Entrance Fees: The garden is open in April and October on Sundays and at Easter; from May to September daily except Mondays and Fridays (2-5pm). Teas are served from May to August at weekends and on Bank Holidays; £2.50, OAP/Students/Children £1.90; Children under 10 free but not admitted at weekends.

Things to look out for:
1   Two love birds in a loggia
2   Heads with two faces, one young the other old
3   Yews in the shape of Sienese sugar loaves
4   A rook on a wheatsheaf
5   A man disguised as a bird
6   A Roman boar hunt

Garden Tour:
The approach to Iford is as idyllic as the garden itself. The lane pitches down from the Bath-Warminster road between high hedges more Dorset than Wiltshire, and as it turns a corner Britannia rears into view on the mediaeval bridge with the garden rising up the hill behind the house. There are pale green willows by the river, the Georgian manor is built of a rich golden limestone and there

are deep green cypresses and splashes of copper red in the gardens. The house was owned by a succession of wealthy clothiers – the Hortons in the Elizabethan period and the Chandlers who gave it a fashionable Palladian front in the mid-eighteenth century. But the first planting on the hillside was carried out by the Gaisfords who owned the house from 1773 to 1853. The great cedar on the hillside walk was planted in 1780 and Thomas Gaisford, Dean of Christ Church, Oxford, planted snowdrops and the unusual martagon lilies in the wild garden and in the woods. The house and grounds were dilapidated by 1899 when the Rooke family sold it to Harold Peto.

Peto was a practising architect working in partnership with the Arts and Crafts expert, Sir Ernest George. They had been influenced by William Morris's craft-centred aesthetic and were responsible for training the young Edwin Lutyens. Much of what Peto achieved at Iford can be seen to have had a profound effect on Lutyens when he came to construct the gardens at Hestercombe in Somerset. 'Architectural Gardens' were all the rage in the 1890s, a combination of buildings and plants, harking back nostalgically to the formal gardens of England's past with their walks, terraces and summer houses. Peto compiled a manuscript, the 'Boke of Iford', in which he wrote: 'Old buildings or fragments of masonry carry one's mind back to the past in a way that a garden of flowers only cannot do. Gardens that are too stony are equally unsatisfactory; it is the combination of the two in just proportion which is the most satisfactory'. At Iford the past is of Italy rather than England where architectural fragments and statuary are dramatised by cypresses, broad walks and pools as if it were a Roman villa garden.

Walk past the main front of the house, through the archway and into the garden. Peto sets the Italian mood by the Loggia with its antique plaques, marble cameos of Roman emperors and Byzantine roundels of animals and birds which appear again on walls throughout the garden. Opposite the Loggia is a semi-circular pool with a river god above a lion mask fountain. Pools, fountains and dripping water are a constant theme of the garden. From this little entrance courtyard you will see the steps to the terraces alongside the house with their dry-stone walls and curving ashlar copings draped with vines and honeysuckle. The first terrace is a good place to see the Elizabethan house onto which the Georgian façade was clamped. It is built of rubble stone with some surviving mullioned windows and a gabled roofline – typical Cotswold vernacular which must have charmed Peto more than the swagger Georgian show front. The second terrace is said to have replaced a chapel and small cloister so Peto gave it a semi-ecclesiastical theme with two Sienese saints in *aediculae* set into the walls. There is a fifteenth-century well head, a pair of marble lions supporting columns of about 1200 and two unusual Janus heads which are Roman terminal posts for marking the boundaries of two properties.

Go up the next flight of steps which is bordered by fragrant lavender and wisteria, turn left and walk towards the small paved court. On your left are the back roof slopes of the house with their beautifully graded stone slates. Walk past the court to the soothing sound of trickling water and make for the Blue Pool on the next level. There is a mill grinding wheel in the pavement here to remind us of past owners, and curious topiary yews clipped into piles of sugar loaves, the crest of the Chigi family of Siena from whom the present owner's grandmother was descended. Don't miss the rather bottom-heavy woman riding a lion on the wall above the pool.

Walk up to the Great Terrace with its colonnade, pillars and sculpture. This was where Dean Gainsford used to prepare his sermons on Summer evenings. Peto paved it with York stone flags but by the 1960s these had decayed and they have been replaced by gravel. To your left is a curved seat marking the formal boundary of the garden with the rustic orchard beyond. The seat is wooden and very comfortable; sit a while to enjoy the views down the length of the terrace and see if you can spot the rook on the wheatsheaf. The well head in front of you comes from a church cloister in Ravenna and dates from 534. Now walk through the colonnade into the Casita enclosure. This has pink marble columns from Verona and an incongruous Cotswold slate roof, but I suspect that clay pantiles, though more in keeping with Italian garden buildings, would have looked garish on this limestone hillside. The planting here is consciously Mediterranean with wisteria, lilies and acanthus. Again there is the refreshing sound of dripping water, this time from an animal spout into a cistern surrounded by pink geraniums in terracotta pots.

Pass the marble statue of a rather epicene youth and head into the woods to the Japanese Garden with its little pagodas, rockwork and pools. Then look up the great staircase climbing into the woods to the column set up to commend Edward VII's efforts to avoid the disaster of the First World War; perhaps an alliance with Germany rather than France might have served his cause more successfully. Under the trees to your right is a statue of Papageno in his bird-catching costume from Mozart's Magic Flute. Go down to the Great Terrace again where there are more fragments and sculptures; take your time and look out for huge terracotta urns, German hounds, a Roman boar hunt and the She Wolf suckling Romulus and Remus. The Lily Pond below once had a colonnade but this was blown down in the 1940s; the figure of the huntsman and his dog is sixteenth century. At the east end of the terrace is an early eighteenth-century Tea House with Ionic pilasters and a conical roof. This still has its original panelling and a chunky fireplace. A particularly satisfying touch is the wooden glazing bars of the sashes which have been left unpainted. Pause here by the balustrade to look across the walls of the Kitchen Garden by the river and the cultivated fields beyond.

The gravelled walk from the Tea House leads through a berberis arbour to Peto's last building, The Cloisters. The building was completed in 1914 and intended as an outdoor museum for those antique fragments which he had not used elsehwere in the garden. The prevailing style of the architecture is late-twelfth-century Romanesque though the main doorway surround is said to have come from Mantua and dates from about 1450. The fragments are arranged chronologically with Classical objects to your left as you enter, a Byzantine section at the east end, a Gothic area to the south and Renaissance sculpture on the west wall. If you visit the garden between June and August you might catch one of the concerts that are staged regularly in The Cloisters.

Finally, walk down the path by the lawn and stop a moment where two paths meet to see the statue of the Dying Gaul and Britannia on the cutwater of the bridge beyond, potent symbols of Peto's dual inspiration for Iford: a love of his native country at a time of national crisis and a passion for Italian antiquities.

Two Gardens of a Golden Afternoon

Hestercombe, Somerset

Theme: Two wildly contrasted gardens: an informal eighteenth-century Arcadian landscape, and a strictly formal Edwardian garden laid out by the brilliant team of Edwin Lutyens and Gertrude Jekyll. Add to this a Victorian ornamental terrace and at Hestercombe you range over three centuries of garden design.

Directions: Hestercombe is four miles from Taunton, close to the village of Cheddon Fitzpaine. Take junction 24 from the M5 on to the A38, drive south to Monkton Elm and then follow the Tourist Information Daisy symbol. You might want to visit Hestercombe in the morning and return to Bath via Iford to see where Lutyens got his inspiration. In any event give yourself at least two hours to enjoy the two gardens at Hestercombe.

Opening Times and Entrance Fees: The gardens are open all year except Christmas Day and Boxing Day (10-6; last entry 5pm); £3.50, Children aged 5-15 £1.00; Children under 5 enter free.

Things to look out for:
1   Fire engines
2   Horticultural hypocausts
3   Patterned pavements
4   An Impressionist's flower border
5   A pink Mausoleum for the studious
6   A Hut for Macbeth's weird sisters

Garden Tour:
     On your approach to the car-park you will see several fire engines as the house and gardens were first leased by Somerset County Fire Brigade when the last member of the Portman family died in 1951. The firemen restored the Edwardian garden in 1973 and the property was eventually bought in 1977. The Hestercombe

Gardens Trust has now been set up to continue the restoration and maintenance of both gardens.

The plain eighteenth-century house was given a complete revamp in 1874-7 and ended up even uglier than before with a tall tower that looks as if it has escaped from a town hall in Normandy. Fortunately our interest is in the gardens laid out after 1903 by Lutyens and Jekyll for the Honourable E W B Portman, and the secret landscape contrived by Coplestone Warre Bamfylde from 1750 to 1785. So walk up to the Victorian terrace below the house and start there.

The top terrace was laid out by Viscount Portman in 1872-7 when he was busy extending the house. It is a perfect example of the Victorians' craze for brilliant colour and bedding plants. The central fountain has been recently restored and the four rectangular beds have been planted up from conventional lists of the time with regimented splashes of royal purple and orange geraniums. It is both instructive and a welcome relief to move from this garish display to Jekyll's paler palette of whites, silvers, greys and purples.

Edwin Lutyens is said to have met Gertrude Jekyll one afternoon at a Surrey tea party. She had taken to gardening because she had ruined her eyesight painting and doing intricate needlework. Most of her gardens combine a close attention to the particular shape and detail of plants with a general impression of the colour sequences which they produce. The Grey Walk is the best place to test out her method, but before you go down to it walk into the Rose Garden to see how Lutyens creates a subtle stone framework of golden Ham Hill ashlar and razor-edged local rubble stone to complement his partner's planting.

Go down the steps noticing how the stones have been laid for colour contrast and texture. Changes of level are a constant feature of Lutyens's plan opening up vistas across the layout. The Rose Garden has a Lutyens-designed seat, the first of many throughout the garden, set within a wych elm arbour that provides a rustic canopy for shelter from either sun or rain. The garden extends in beds of dwarf roses to a balustrade beyond which is the Vale of Taunton Deane with the Black Down Hills in the distance. But what entices you down to the paved terrace and the view is the sound of water trickling from an unknown source. At the balustrade you command the entire length of the West Water Garden with its rill or canal, a stone-edged watercourse which branches at two points into owl-like double circles. It may be wishful thinking on my part, but these remind me of the curious strainer arches in the crossing at Wells Cathedral. The channel is bushy with purple irises and other water plants; the silver stone paths contrast with the green lawns of the terrace and directly below you are retaining walls and rusticated doorways clothed with figs and vines. Looking out from this vantage point you can see the Pergola which marks the southern boundary of the formal area and there is an oblique glimpse of the Great Plat to the left. But still the water source is hidden, so walk down two levels to find it.

A mill wheel grinding stone is set in the steps as you descend to the West Water Garden, a design feature which Lutyens must have learnt from Harold Peto at Iford. Walk through the archway and you are drawn to the arcing stream of water issuing from the mouth of a water god above a concave niche with a moon pool set below. Like a Green Man he peers out through a tangled mass of vines. On either side of the niche are circular recesses ready for busts or small statues. Now walk back up to the Grey Walk. Here you can sense the influence of Jekyll's close friend, the Impressionist watercolourist, Hercules Brabazon, who painted like Turner with an emphasis on colour and light. To appreciate the planting as Jekyll would have seen it with her myopia, you need to study the plants closely to enjoy their individual forms and then look across the borders with half-shut eyes to perceive the Impressionistic effect produced by the co-ordinated blocks of colour. From the Grey Walk there is a spectacular view of the whole layout with the Great Plat below, the Pergola beyond and the symmetrical Water Gardens to east and west.

Moon steps give access to the Plat at each corner and the pattern is of a great cross with a diamond at the centre producing triangular-shaped beds. The planting of the beds softens the edges of the silver pavements while in contrast the paved walks in the grass are sharply defined. Here the planting is not original, but enjoy the beds and the borders before you make for the south-west corner steps. There are square tanks at the end of both Water Gardens, fed by the canal-rills; these are dappled with lush water lilies. Then the Pergola strides along the southern axis in alternate round and square rubble stone piers supporting an open roof of arched beams. Vines and honeysuckle climb up the piers, drifts of lavender add colour to the borders and the pavement is deliberately laid with irregular-shaped flags to give variety. Walk towards the port-hole opening for views out to the fields at the south-east corner and then enter the East Water Garden. If you look down into the rill you will see stones laid on edge in the water course to aid a rippling flow and free-standing stone columns like hypocausts supporting the flags of the stone edging. Make for the moon pool with its woman water head and then through the archway, up to the Rotunda Court.

The Rotunda is stonier than the rest of the garden with golden ashlar dressings to the silvery local rubble stone walls. Although this is a formal enclosure with pedimented niche and stone piers, which once supported small statues of cherubs holding baskets, there are still views back to the top terrace, down to the East Water Garden and out to the Orangery. The ingenuity of the garden plan is apparent here as the axis now veers off to the north-west and steps lead down to the Orangery and the Dutch Garden beyond. It is as if the architectural formality of the Rotunda has consciously prepared the visitor for the Renaissance detail of the Orangery with its carved swags of fruit and wall of Palladian windows. Further along the terrace the steps ascend to the Dutch Garden with its low retaining walls, stone piers, and beds centred by terracotta vases. Here there is silvery stachys edging to the borders, yuccas which give vertical emphasis, santolinas, lavender and fuschias which provide enlivening splashes of deep red. The whole layout evokes the golden afternoon glow of patrician Edwardian England before the horrors of the trenches decimated an entire generation.

Through a Chinese-style doorway in the Dutch Garden you will see the eighteenth-century garden up the valley behind the house. The Georgian pleasure grounds were laid out by Coplestone Warre Bamfylde who had inherited the estate in 1750. He was an amateur artist and close friend of Henry Hoare of Stourhead. He painted several views of Hoare's famous landscape and his layout at Hestercombe was obviously influenced by his neighbour's. Bamfylde planted up the sides of his long, narrow valley with trees through which he threaded winding walks dotted with surprise garden buildings. Just as at Stourhead, from each building there was a contrived view either across the valley or down to the lake in the valley bottom below. But whereas Hoare's layout had a distinct iconographical programme based on Virgil's *Aeneid*, Bamfylde's appears to have been purely eclectic with buildings in all manner of architectural styles.

Much of what Bamfylde achieved has now been revealed by a fairly drastic but wholly successful scheme of woodland clearance. The lake has been dredged and its contours reclaimed, areas of woodland have been cut back on the valley slopes to reinstate the original lines of the tree planting and several of the ornamental buildings have been restored. Although the landscape is still under restoration, a clearly defined walk will take you past the major sites. The most atmospheric is the Witch or Root House made from tree trunks, bark and thatch. This was seen by Edward Knight, Bamfylde's brother-in-law, when he visited Hestercombe in 1761. Knight made a list of the garden features in his notebook which includes an octagonal summer house, Chinese and Gothic seats and a 'Tent' with an open view of the Taunton Vale. This last may well have been a Turkish tent popular in other gardens of the period.

From the Witch House there is a view across the valley to the Waterfall which Bamfylde built in 1762 after seeing one at William Shenstone's gardens at The Leasowes, near Halesowen. Henry Hoare was so impressed by the cascade that he asked Bamfylde to design another for him at Stourhead. The Hestercombe Waterfall is fed by a brick and stone leat extending for three hundred yards in a sinuous stream curling around the hillside.

Past the Witch House you come to an austere Doric Temple built in about 1775 and perched high on the hillside commanding a view down to the lake and the Vale beyond. Further on there is the site of an Alcove Seat, the Box Pond and a Charcoal Burner's Camp. My favourite building is the curious pink Mausoleum for which Edward Knight recorded precise measurements in 1761.

It is like a piece of two-dimensional stage scenery with urn-topped
piers, pyramid and sinister rusticated archway giving access to a
small, gloomy chamber. Below the pyramid is an inscription on
slate which perfectly sums up the atmosphere of relaxed intellectual
retirement encouraged by Bamfylde's Romantic landscape:

> Happy the Man who to the Shades retires
> Whom Nature charms, and whom the Muse inspires,
> Blest whom the Sweets of home-felt Quiet please:
> But far more blest, who Study joins with Ease.

The Engineer and the Cottage Artist

Great Chalfield Manor and Garden, Wiltshire

Theme: This is a garden where the adjoining house is as important as the plants and layout, where the vistas are contrived to frame the house and its grounds as if in a series of watercolour studies. The house is a mediaeval manor dating from 1465-80 and the garden was designed by the owner, Robert Fuller, and his artist-gardener, Alfred Parsons, between 1909 and 1911.

Directions: Great Chalfield Manor is one mile west of Broughton Gifford between Bradford-on-Avon and Melksham. Make for Bradford-on-Avon on the A363 and, before entering the town, turn left on the B3109 to Bradford Leigh. Turn right at the pub and head for the Manor on a minor lane which skirts fields of wheat. The Manor is surprisingly unsigned for a National Trust house and appears quite suddenly around a bend in the lane. Park opposite the entrance on the grass verge as cars are not allowed in the grounds.

Opening Times and Entrance Fees: The Manor and Garden are open from 1 April to 29 October, Tuesday to Thursday . Entrance to the Manor is by guided tour only at the following times: 12.15; 2.15; 3.00; 3.45 and 4.30, price £3.60. The garden is part of the Quiet Garden movement and used for prayer and meditation on the first Tuesday of each month, except January and August, from 10-3pm, with a service in the church at 1pm. For more information on the Quiet Garden Trust, which lists 77 gardens in the UK, call: 01753 643050.

Things to look out for:
1   Yews in the shape of jelly moulds
2   A moat with only two sides
3   A mulberry
4   Stone monsters and a monkey
5   Geriatric carp
6   Peep-hole masks

House and Garden Tour:

As entrance to both garden and manor house at Great Chalfield is on a single ticket it is worth arriving in time for one of the guided tours. These take only 45 minutes and give you a real sense of the families who have owned the place from the fifteenth century – the Tropnells, Eyres, Hanhams, Halls, Neales and latterly the Fullers. The mediaeval house was extensively restored and parts were rebuilt between 1905 and 1912 by the local Arts and Crafts architect, Sir Harold Brakspear. Fortunately he was given a complete set of survey drawings of the house as recorded in 1836, and with these was able to achieve a sympathetic and scholarly restoration. One of the pleasures of the tour is spotting what is Mediaeval original and what is fake Edwardian. Don't miss the strange peephole masks in the Hall and the arched wind braces in the timber roofs, original in the North Bedroom, Brakspear copies in the Solar.

The house is guarded on the north by a moat green with duckweed, bushy with bullrushes and coloured by purple loosestrife. Behind it the house rears up like some ideal English manor out of a Pinewood historical drama with the tall gabled roof of the Great Hall immediately visible in the centre. The façade looks almost symmetrical with two oriel windows at each end and there are crouching beasts and armoured soldiers on the gable apexes. To the left is the miniature parish church of All Saints with its delicate, crocketed bellcote and a textured interior which, happily, the Victorians forgot to scrape.

If you toured the house you will have seen tantalising glimpses of the gardens through mullioned windows to the south and east. They were laid out by Robert Fuller with advice from the Newbury firm of Parsons and Partridge. Fuller won a gold medal for electrical engineering at Faraday House in 1896 and then spent the rest of his working life with the Avon Rubber Company in Melksham. He took over the house from a tenant of his father's who left in 1905. By 1909 the restoration of the house was well under way and Fuller's thoughts turned to an appropriate garden setting.

Alfred Parsons was best known at this time for his landscape watercolours and his book illustrations, which included the 1880 edition of *The Wild Garden*. A founder member of the Art Workers

Guild, he had created formal gardens at Wightwick Manor just outside Birmingham and remodelled the Provost's garden at Worcester College, Oxford planting the borders with old-fashioned flowers. In 1909 he was just beginning to work with Captain Croker Ives Partridge. Parsons was responsible for the designs and planting plans while Partridge looked after the administration of the projects. The firm was to be paid 50 guineas a year for three years to create the Great Chalfield layout and carry out the planting. The construction work was to cost £250, and £100 was earmarked for plants. The firm's house style was a modern re-interpretation of English country and cottage gardens combined with the more formal architectural elements of the Elizabethan plesaunce – terraces, raised walks, banqueting pavilions and gazebos – the perfect garden for a mediaeval manor house.

Walk through the gate in the wall to the left of the house and look up at the bearded face under the oriel window as you follow the path to the Lawn. Here there was originally a medlar, now replaced by a mulberry and walnut, successors to Parsons's planting. There are two jelly-mould yew houses here, which on Parsons's 1909 plan were simply two arches of topiary, the raised walk is on your left with the main lawn which was meant for a tennis court, the ornamental pond and fountain, and the garden house at the right-hand corner. Apart from the removal of the tennis court little has changed since Parsons devised the plans and there is still continuity in the planting as he used a small range of species. The same roses are used throughout the garden – Bennett's Seedling and climbing Madame Caroline Testout with Alister Stella Gray planted on the house and garden walls. In the Church Border to your left there is a subdued colour scheme of lily-flowered tulips in the Spring then chrysanthemums, sweet rocket and Autumn cyclamen.

The Lawn Border at the eastern boundary of the garden comes into its own in Summer with dramatic colour blends of herbaceous geraniums, limonium, centaureas and Italian White sunflowers. The Garden House is built of local limestone with a steep conical roof of carefully graded Cotswold stone slates. Brakspear prepared the working drawings for the building which is part summer-house and part gazebo. Such sixteenth and seventeenth-century

55

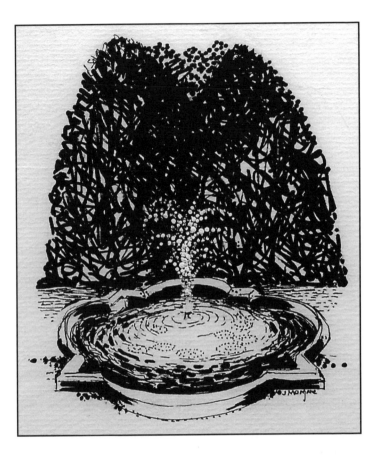

'neighbourhood watch' houses are common in this part of Wiltshire though they usually command village streets. To the moat on the south it has two storeys with a wide four-light mullioned window at lawn level and a storage room below. At this point there is a descent to the moat and a walk along the southern boundary path. This is where you will sometimes catch one of those overweight and antiquated carp surfacing through the weeds like miniature nuclear submarines. When you have taken in the views of the Aster, Bastion, Summer and Dovecote Borders across the Orchard with the south front of the house behind, retrace your steps to enjoy in more detail the planting of the individual borders.

The Top Terrace opposite the Garden House is planted with self-sown rock roses and verbascums. There are maidenhair spleenwort ferns and ivy-leaved toadflax on its dry stone retaining wall which gives a stony backdrop to the Aster Border where various Michaelmas daisies have been grouped with more herbaceous geraniums and pulmonarias to give Spring and Summer interest to this essentially autumnal border. Further on, the moat steps lead down to the Orchard where a fascinating range of bulbs planted by Parsons flower in the Spring, including some rare old narcissus cultivars. These are followed by homely cow parsley and natural meadow flowers, then in the Summer the old apple trees are smothered in rambler roses.

The south-facing Paved Court is bordered on its west side by Brakspear's timber-framed range supported on posts under which there is a loggia. The foundations of a range of buildings which once enclosed this courtyard to the south can still be seen, and a circular flower bed has been formed on what was probably the foundations of a Norman defensive tower or dovecote, hence the names of the borders. Correspondence between Fuller and Parsons reveals how they agonised about the size of the beds in the courtyard. Parsons was obsessed with making sure that the rose bushes had enough room to grow. Today they are planted with the polyanthus hybrid rose Nathalie Nypels while luscious pink and red climbing roses entwine the timber posts.

Robert Fuller gave Great Chalfield to the National Trust in 1943, but his daughter's family still lives in the house so it is a living home and not a showpiece museum. Patsy and Robert Floyd, together with their garden expert Neil Brocklehurst, have succeeded in maintaining much of what Parsons designed and planted back in 1909. Patsy Floyd also runs a 'Garden Party' business which takes small groups on private garden explorations in the area. For further information about these tours contact Patsy Floyd and Susan Chivers at Great Chalfield Manor, Melksham, Wiltshire SN12 8NJ; Tel: 01225 782239/Fax: 01225 783379. Finally, *The Bell* on the Common at nearby Broughton Gifford is handy for good pub food.

A Whimsical Garden in the Prince Charles Manner

Barnsley House Garden, Gloucestershire

Theme: Rosemary Verey would never do anything so brash as to advertise her friendship with her near neighbour, Prince Charles, but she has in fact often advised him on his garden at Highgrove and he on hers at Barnsley. Together they have evolved an essentially modern style, witty, allusive, full of references to the past, but also strongly ecological, even politically correct, with their rich 'potagers' where old and exotic new fruit and vegetables combine beauty with utility. This is the new organic chic. So if Highgrove's gates are closed, sample its style and atmosphere at Barnsley and see if you can pick out the Princely touches, just that little bit coy as well as worthy.

Directions: Barnsley is on the B4425 from Cirencester to Burford, about 2 miles north-east of Cirencester. From Bath the most picturesque route is via the A46/A433 to Cirencester. As you approach Cirencester take the ring road and follow signs to Burford. Your arrival in Barnsley is signalled by dry stone walls and Cotswold stone cottages with an olive green livery on windows and doors. Barnsley House is signposted to your right just along the main street.

Opening Times and Entrance Fees: The garden is open on Monday, Wednesday, Thursday & Saturday (10am-5.30pm) all year except for January, Christmas Day & Boxing Day. £3.50; concessions: £2.50.

Things to look out for:
1   Two temples – one Gothick, the other Classical
2   Garden maids with flower baskets
3   A female Phantom of the Opera
4   Frogs spouting water at two rams
5   A princely potager
6   A nasturtium arbour with hanging marrows

Garden Tour:

Barnsley House was built by Brereton Bourchier in 1697; you will see the date and his initials carved over the front door. By 1762 the house had become a Rectory and in 1767 Charles Coxwell was given the living. He began by building a high stone wall around the property and then added the Gothick summerhouse to the garden, which he called his 'arbour'. The 1820 terraces to the front of the house were laid out by the Rev. Richard Musgrave and the trees on the drive planted by Canon Howman in the nineteenth century. But the major features of the garden behind the house belong to David and Rosemary Verey who have created, in her own words, 'a country garden with formal and historical features but overflowing with plants and interest'. The formal garden area, small and intimate, is divided from the 'Potager' or kitchen garden by a mud-plashed country track. There is interest all year round, but the most spectacular colours appear in the Spring and in May and June when the laburnum flowers and Summer perennials reach their peak. As Rosemary writes: 'it has become eclectic in design and atmosphere'. This conscious eclecticism has been inspired both by the writings of garden theorists such as Gervase Markham, William Robinson and Vita Sackville-West and by the various owners of Barnsley. So the Knot Garden is a seventeenth-century design that Bourchier might have planted in a formal mood and the Wilderness is a Romantic complement to Coxwell's Gothick Summerhouse.

You begin your tour in the Greenhouse Yard which gives onto the main lawn in front of the house. The manor is built of that silvery Cotswold limestone of the area with three gables, a graded stone slate roof and later 1820s wing. The path to the shop on your right is flanked by a shrub border and an ingenious bed of lozenge-shaped box hedging with all kinds of herbs sprouting from the diamonds and triangles. All the borders in the garden are well labelled and there is a succession of of flowering shrubs here as the seasons change – hellebores in the early Spring, then paeonies, narcissus and tulips growing through drifts of forget-me-nots in April and May. Then come foxgloves and ferns and the rambler rose 'Wickwar' which covers the wall.

The borders under the house have climbing plants chosen for their scent and cover. The old Wisteria sinensis flowers in May and there are two evergreens – Hebe speciosa and Phillyrea angustifolia – which soften the outline of the stone walls all year round. At the corner of the house you will find the Verandah Terrace and the Knot Garden. The verandah is in Regency Gothic style and was built by Musgrave in the 1820s. One of the earliest Verey plantings was the strawberry vine, Vitis 'Fragola', recommended by Vita Sackville-West, which climbs the south-west-facing wall. Here there are teak chairs designed by Rosemary's son, Charles, so sit and enjoy the Knot Garden and the views across the lawn to the Wilderness where you might spot a sinister figure lurking in the foliage.

The Knot Garden dates from the early 1970s and its design was taken from the seventeenth-century gardener, Gervase Markham's *La Maison Rustique* and 'the true Lover's Knott' in a book of 1664. The interweaving patterns are of different kinds of clipped box and there are four golden hollies, Ilex 'Golden King', which mark the corners. Walk from the Knot towards the Wilderness and you will discover the Hunting Lady, one of several statues designed for the garden after 1972 by Simon Verity. Dressed for the hunt with high stock, riding crop and a greyhound, she seems to have stepped out of a society painting by John Singer Sargent, but there is a strange René Magritte touch to her face which is completely covered by a netted veil. The Wilderness is for exploration rather than for browsing. In Spring you will find snowdrops, daffodils, camassias (my favourites), snakeshead fritillaries and in its recesses a deliciously dank, unheated, old-fashioned swimming pool. This is one feature of Barnsley which Highgrove is most unlikely to have imitated. How often, one wonders, do the Vereys take a plunge?

On your left is the Gothick Summerhouse, or Mrs Coxwell's 'alcove', of panelled Gothick arches, battlements and pinnacles. Romantic seats like these need good evergreen planting to produce a pleasing gloom and the Summerhouse is shaded by a 160-year-old holm oak and a yew hedge clipped into more battlements. At the foot of the oak in Autumn there are clumps of Cyclamen

hederifolium. To the left of the holm oak is an L-shaped bed of sturdy Rosa rugosa which had enormous hips when I was in the garden in late Autumn. In the middle of the bed is a young mulberry which the seventeenth-century horticulturalist John Evelyn said was the best guide as to when delicate plants could be put outside – not until the mulberry flowers.

Walk past the Summerhouse and down towards the Frog Fountain. This is an extraordinarily powerful sculpture and water feature designed by Simon Verity with two Cotswold rams fighting each other while four frogs spout water into a basin. From here you can look back up the length of the Grass Walk to the Classical Temple and enjoy the left-hand border which was planted in Gertrude Jekyll style with controlled colour gradations.

Now dive into the Laburnum Tunnel where there is a column with a copper plate inscribed with Evelyn's words: 'As no man be very miserable that is Master of a Garden here; so will no man ever be happy who is not sure of a Garden here after'. Next comes the Lime Walk with a wall on your right of climbing roses, honeysuckles and clematis. With the Frog Fountain still in earshot and several seats shaded by the trees this is the perfect place to sit, as John Evelyn did in his 'cabinets' at Sayes Court, Deptford, and take in the sights and sounds of the garden. On my last visit the house was being used for corporate entertainment and smoky Jazz played by a trio on the Terrace wafted across the lawn to my Lime Walk seat.

Guarding the wrought-iron gate to the Potager are stone ladies with wide brimmed hats, yearning looks and baskets of flowers. These have the same attenuated elegance of the Hunting Lady and are again by Simon Verity. At this point duck into the muddy lane and cross to the Potager with its geometrically planned beds, brick paths and well dressed scarecrow – look for the mouse scrambling up his trouser leg. Interspersed amongst the vegetables are foxgloves, sweet peas and sunflowers and an extraordinary nasturtium tunnel. Double back to the main garden and then head right for the Classical Temple via the dwarf box hedge walk ingeniously planted with pots of lavender in the centre.

The Tuscan Doric Temple was moved to Barnsley from Fairford Park in 1962 and sited in front of an existing pool that was made in 1954. As you walk through the gates you might notice the osiers on either side which have clematis climbing up them. There are marsh marigolds and Iris sibirica edging the pool and the corner beds have bergenias, day lilies and junipers. The Temple is framed on one side by a silver birch with lower golden-leaved privet, and on the other by an ash, a quince, and an old fig. More clematis and roses cover the wall and all around you will see pot plants which are moved about the enclosure as they come into bloom.

Retrace your steps to the Rock Rose Path with its goblet-shaped Irish yews and play hopscotch over the roses on the crazy paving. From here you can examine the four parterre beds which have a succession of plants flowering for each season; look particularly at the corners to enjoy the careful structure of the planting. And before you leave the garden don't miss the Grotto in a conservatory which links the manor house with 'The Close' where Rosemary Verey now lives. If you are hungry, the coyly named *Village Pub* on the main street serves delicious food and on your journey home you might think of stopping off to see the arboretum at Westonbirt which is a must in leafy Autumn.